Suellen,

Thank you for being my mentor, encourager and a ... You are truly a blessing in my life. I love you dearly.

Please feel free to share this with anyone you believe may be touched by ...

All my love.

Love,
Aka-Tanya

*Remember those who are in prison, as though in prison with them, and those who are mistreated, since you also are in the body.*

Hebrews 13:3

*I needed clothes and you clothed me, I was sick and you looked after me, I was in prison and you came to visit me.'*

Matthew 25:36

*This book is dedicated to the women at Coffee Creek Correctional Facility, not only those who provided quilts but all those we have met on the inside who have shared a bit of their lives with us.*

**Kyle Black**
*resident of Coffee Creek Correctional Facility*

© 2016 - Fran Howard / Freedom in the Son (FITS)

All rights reserved. No part of this book may be used or reproduced by any means, graphic, electronic, or mechanical, including photocopying, recording, taping or by any information storage retrieval system without the written permission of the publisher except in the case of brief quotations embodied in critical articles and reviews.

*Information / Media:*

**Freedom in the Son (FITS)**
fran.howard@comcast.net

ISBN 978-0-9970008-1-8 - *softcover*
ISBN 978-0-9970008-2-5 - *ebook*

*Cover Illustration* - Tammy Rodgers
*Book Design* - www.timmyroland.com

# The Quilt

stories compiled by
**Fran Howard** & Friends

YACOB & TOMAS
WORLDWIDE

*The Quilt*

# Contents

**Forward** .................................... *i*
**Introduction** .............................. *iv*

**The Stories**

    Neva ........................................ 1
    Tanya ....................................... 5
    Danielle .................................. 13
    Becky ..................................... 19
    Tammy ..................................... 23
    Jacqueline ................................ 31
    Nancy ..................................... 41
    Lakisha ................................... 47
    Rose ...................................... 55
    Fran ...................................... 59

**Addendum** ................................. 69

**Did You Know?** ........................... 74

**About Freedom in the Son (FITS)** ........ 77

*The Quilt*

# Foreword

Can you have fun inside a women's prison? Absolutely! Can you have dynamic worship inside a women's prison? Yes, the best worship, ever! Can you have creative workshops, learn from inspiring speakers, hear amazing stories of faith and deliverance? Yes! Can you see lives changed and transformed by the power and hope of faith in Jesus? For sure! How could you not get hooked on prison ministry?

I stumbled into prison ministry accidentally, never dreaming that it would capture my heart and vision for years. Over 25 years ago, my husband and I were publishing Virtue Magazine, a magazine for Christian women, and we received a letter from a woman inmate. She wrote to tell us how God had used some of the articles to inspire her and give her hope. We printed her letter in the "Letters Column" and began receiving gift subscriptions from our subscribers for women in prison.

At the time, we were doing "Virtue Live" conferences for women with the idea of presenting a live magazine in a weekend conference. We began hosting an annual "Virtue Live" conference in the women's prison, taking a team of about twenty volunteers to lead a weekend conference. We prayed and planned for each annual conference, and for many of us, it was the highlight of our year, a life-changing experience. We did this for 17 years.

Shortly after we started doing these conferences in the women's prison, I met Fran Howard, who had become a full-time volunteer chaplain for the women's prison. Fran—now nearly 85 years young with an infectious laugh—is short in stature but with a heart as big as the world. After retiring from teaching at George Fox University and Willamette University, Fran began spending her retirement years to lead Freedom in the Son, a volunteer ministry for women in prison, as well as being a support when the women leave prison.

Real heroes can be hard to spot. They can be like stealth weapons, or special forces that work behind the scenes, unheralded and in many cases, hidden. We may not even know their names as they don't usually have a marketing agent. Yet they live their common lives with such a radical sense of giving; of sacrifice, that when our lives touch theirs we cannot stay the same. They show us, more than tell us. Fran Howard is such a person, and one of my heroines of the faith. There are many layers and aspects to Fran Howard's life of ministry. Fran has been a spiritual mother to literally thousands of women, caring and listening and inspiring them to trust Jesus with their whole lives. Fran's ministry has not only helped the women inside prison and their families (as well as after incarceration), but she and her team have helped many others who have come alongside the ministry of Freedom in the Son.

Prison ministry is not an easy ministry. Our conference was an annual one; Fran Howard and her team have been there for the women inmates day after day . . . year after year, encouraging, praying, teaching, rejoicing, and weeping with the set-backs.

I pray that as you read this book and listen to the stories of women who have been through difficult trials, you will also see your own story here, because we all go through hard times, and we all need a Savior. And we all can answer the call to go to the "least of these," as Fran Howard and many other dear friends have, and do whatever we can do, wherever we are. It doesn't have to be much: Simple awareness. Prayer. A financial gift. A gift of time to write a letter, or to be a mentor to women as they re-enter society. And more than anything, to realize that each life is significant. And to learn to listen without judging, knowing that Jesus can Redeem all, if we dare to offer our whole selves to him.

Fran's example has shown that to be successfully effective for God in the world is to be in God for the world. It is that heart of prayer—that waiting, listening, staying in there in a truly difficult ministry field that has helped Fran and Freedom in the Son to be a hopeful and beautiful light for God in a hard place.

Nancie Carmichael
*Author / Speaker, 2016*

*The Quilt*

# Introduction

In 1984 I was invited to join my friend, Madeline Manning Mims for a weekend in the women's prison in Gig Harbor, Washington. Madeline would be singing and sharing her experience as a 4 time Olympic runner and I would just come along to carry her CD's and spend some time with her. Little did I know that the Father had a plan for me that would send me to many prisons throughout the world.

As I sat on the floor outside the chapel residents began to come up and talk with me. I would listen and before long my heart was softening and being drawn to these ladies and wondering how I could help them. There seemed to be such a spirit of unworthiness and no hope within them . At the same time I was reminded of the promise of God which states that "Jesus Christ is the hope of glory" and I began to get excited with the prospect of going home to Oregon to plan how I could be involved in bringing hope to those ladies in prison.

At the time I was in my 15th year of teaching and coaching at Willamette University. One of the sports I coached during the school year was women's softball and in the summer I coached a softball team sponsored by the First Church of the Nazarene. The women on this team became my first volunteers as opportunity arose for us to go into the women's prison to compete with the team inside. Those 14 women softball players faithfully went into the prison for over 4 years – not only to play ball but to share their expertise in other areas of life. Our team consisted of an electrician, accountant, math teacher, two physical education teachers, social service workers, a church secretary, an elementary

## The Quilt

school teacher, and several office secretaries. During the time we played together we became know as the FITS (Freedom in the Son) prison ministry team and had the fun and privilege of playing in a number of prisons in the Northwest. God used the medium of sports to open the door to sharing the life and love of Jesus with hurting women and that became our mission statement as we incorporated and became a non-profit ministry.

I discovered the verse in Hebrews 13:3 that exhorts us to "Remember those who are in prison as though you lived among them and those who have been abused as though you too had suffered abuse." We sought to live Christ inside the prison – to take his light into the darkness so women could experience His love and be set free. Living among them meant sharing our spiritual gifting with them so we began to mentor, help with the learning of math, instruct in physical fitness and well being, help them discover how to forgive others , grieve their losses and work toward becoming constructive members of their communities when they were released. Today, 31 years later four of the original volunteers (softball players) are still serving the women in prison as they teach bible studies, mentor, help prepare for pre and post release and serve as friends to those who once were without hope and looked down on by our society.

The stories of some of these women who Christ set free follow this introduction. It is our prayer that this book may give you new insight into the power of God to change lives.

*To God be the glory.*
*Great things He has done.*

*So loved He the world that*
*He sent us His Son.*

# The Stories

## GOD OPENS PRISON DOORS

# Neva

I grew up in a dysfunctional and physically-abusive family. We never talked about God, and I never heard about Jesus. Everyone, even in my extended family, was a drug addict, alcoholic or both. When I was in third grade I started drinking, smoking and shoplifting. At 9-years old, I was arrested for assault with a deadly weapon. At 13, I started doing heroin. Shortly after that, I committed my first act of armed robbery. At age 15 my father emancipated me. I had no desire to change my behavior or my life.

I was 35-years-old when I was finally arrested for armed robbery and sentenced to 40 months in prison where I continued to use drugs and make new drug-addict friends. After my release, I got pregnant, staying clean-and-sober for 9 months. After my daughter was born, I began the cycle of drugs and armed robbery all over again until I was arrested. I surrendered my 7-month-old baby to my cousin.

Depressed and angry at facing what I believed was 32 years in prison, I wished I were dead. Spending just under a year in county jail, on the way to the courtroom for sentencing I said my first prayer: "God, if you are really there, then you know I can't do 32 years. But I can do 20 years, and I will do it for you." Leaving the court room that day, sentenced to exactly 20 years in prison, I knew God was for real!

Still, there I was once again: sitting in a cell and at the bottom of the pit. I was angry, hurt, and desperate for my life to be different.

# The Quilt

Thinking about ending it all that day, I attended another church service held in the jail. Yet later, sent to the women's prison in Salem, I once again forgot all about Jesus. It was easier to just fit in with all the other inmates. One day another resident invited me to attend a church service where I was introduced to the FITS volunteers. They welcomed me with open arms. They didn't care that it was my second time in prison. They didn't ask me about my crime or how many people I had hurt in my past—and most importantly, they weren't afraid of me. They told me they loved me, they smiled when they saw me, and gave me a hug.

I began attending the FITS services regularly. When I was depressed they prayed with me and talked with me about the love of Jesus Christ. If I missed a week of Bible study, they asked about me and sent me messages that they missed me. Every week they were there to encourage and share the Word of God. They taught me through the Word of God how to be a better person and how to share the good news with others. I know the FITS volunteers were put in my life to guide me and teach me about the love of Jesus Christ and what he has done for me. If they had not shown up every week, every Thanksgiving and every Christmas, I would have given up a long time ago.

I was baptized during my stay at the Oregon Women's Correctional Center in Salem on September 2, 2001 by the FITS team. My life has changed so much that I wake up with a smile and I am grateful to be alive. I have become a part of the FITS family. Since I was released in April, 2015, I have attended the FITS retreats and leadership conference. I plan to move to Salem so I can be more involved in the FITS ministries and support groups. A car is awaiting me when I arrive – an answer to prayer for help in transportation. Reconciliation is taking place between myself and my three children. God is so faithful. I am blessed.

*Neva*

### A REFUGE IN THE TIME OF STORM

# Tanya

As a child, I was repeatedly sexually abused by an older cousin, but when I finally told my family about it several years later, they took sides and offered no help or consolation. Turning to my youth group leader for comfort and safety, he responded sternly and harshly, "it is your duty as a Christian to forgive him," leaving me traumatized. I left the church, alone and angry. I became angry at all Christians.

My family continued to take sides on whether I should have told about my cousin's abuse, but no one ever asked me if I was okay. I wasn't. I tried to understand my family, my fears, myself. My mother, a prescription addict, and my brother, an alcoholic, caused me to go searching for some kind of crutch for my own pain. I started pursuing metaphysics, crystals, tarot cards, the I Ching, avurvedic healing and witchcraft. Eventually, I convinced myself that pursuing these things, I was using love and positive energy to help others and make myself a better person. My anger at Christians increased and I even found delight in challenging their beliefs.

As I reached my mid- twenties, I married and gave birth to a beautiful daughter. Her name was Harmony. She was my light, but I was constantly reading self-help books, searching for more light, and dabbling in alternative beliefs and practices. I had a huge hole inside and a wound very deep. What was life all about? Who

## The Quilt

was God? A divorce after just a year of marriage left me unsettled and lost. I battled depression through the following years, and was constantly moving or changing jobs. It was as if I was far away from home, but I didn't know where home was. I wondered: Who was I? Who was God? What was life all about?

I had avoided alcohol for many years, but never forgotten the way it made me feel. Eventually, I began drinking again; one beer one day, then two the next. Ashamed because alcoholism ran in my family, I hid the evidence. I grew depressed and withdrawn as the use of alcohol grew more frequent, and I struggled with my identity and purpose. I began to feel even more disconnected, isolated—and eventually suicidal. I knew I was an alcoholic and I was going to ruin my daughter's life. I felt so disconnected and isolated. When an overwhelming feeling of uselessness made me give up, I knew I needed to get Harmony to a safe place.

The morning of May 19, 2001, I got in my car with my daughter and headed to a friend's place at the Oregon coast. A feeling of utter desperation and lack of control had its grip on me. I knew that I was drunk, and that I needed help. I stopped the car and cried out to God. I didn't use my tarot cards or crystals. I didn't try to contact spirit guides. I remembered the God of my childhood and begged for help. Time just stopped as someone tapped on my window and yelled through the glass, asking if I was all right. But I felt exposed, as if they would see how awful I was inside, so I quickly drove away.

My next memory is waking in the hospital, my mother standing over me. All she said to me was that Harmony was dead. Then I slipped back under sedation. Due to my injuries I was kept heavily sedated for days. By the time I regained consciousness my family was gone. Broken physically and emotionally, and near death myself, I realized slowly that I had caused the death of my only child. I was alone. I knew my life was over. I knew I would be blamed and hated—and that I deserved it. I knew I had brought incredible pain and loss to many besides myself. I knew I would go to prison. I understood that I had lost everything.

Strangely however, I was calm—and the fear was gone. I knew God had spared me from a fate worse than death: to be eternally separated from him. I believe that surely, I would have gone to hell for my blasphemy. But the hand of God touched me in that horrendous accident and began a new work.

Four months later I began my 8 1/2 year stay in the Oregon corrections system where I met the ladies from FITS. Fran, Jeannie, Pam and Dee have all touched my life. They have gently guided me and molded my faith in the Lord, in a future with hope, and in God's love for me. Jeannie met faithfully with me weekly for many years throughout my incarceration guiding me through the slow growth of my faith. It was so different from my childhood. I began to really know God and trust Jesus. I put my trust in Jesus as my Lord and Savior. Of course, I had many demons to face during my incarceration: plagued by shame and guilt, I battled with forgiveness—not the forgiveness offered by others, but the ability or willingness to forgive myself. I remember telling Jeannie it doesn't say anywhere in the Bible that I have to forgive myself. She always smiled and prayed with me. I still haven't found it but I am seeing myself through new eyes now.

The kind of patient sharing and love that the FITS ladies offered changed my direction. Though I faced many demons and was plagued by shame and guilt, today, I know that I am redeemed. Although I would not say it was a good experience, today, I am grateful and blessed for the years I spent inside prison that offered time to grow my relationship with Jesus Christ. Of course, I've had my troubles since leaving prison and adjusting to life outside. I am still trying to figure out who I am now, if I am not Harmony's mother. Although most of my family has not communicated with me since I became incarcerated, I have been offered tremendous support and love and fellowship from the FITS ladies, now on

# The Quilt

the outside of those concrete walls. Married now, with Jesus as an active source of love in both my husband's and my own life, I'm sober and embrace life from a new perspective of redemption.

Every year since my release I attend the FITS retreat at the Oregon coast: an amazing experience: to relax, learn, and pray with the ladies who have become my new family and support system. In that place I am always moved by the Holy Spirit. The FITS volunteers are still with me as friends and mentors. In June, 2013, I was set free from alcoholism as the women prayed for me at the Happy Camp retreat. Always a refreshing renewal of relationship, they are a reminder that I was given the gift of salvation and forgiveness. Now, with a wonderful husband, sober, and learning to embrace life, I understand that I can overcome even in the darkest of times. God continually shows me his love and forgiveness as I embrace beauty and love in the face of trials.

> *"Yet in all things we are more than conquerors through Him who loved us."*
> Romans 8:37

*Tanya, Devin & Milo*

FREEDOM IN THE SON

*Toni*

# The Quilt

*Toni*

*Toni*

## HE SEES EVERY TEAR THAT FALLS

# Danielle

Life before prison was essentially a prison in itself. Before September 2, 2012 I had lived a life with addictions, chaos, brokenness, abuse and desperation. I didn't care how much my actions hurt other people. With no accountability to anyone, I had no sense of direction. I was angry at the world. I remember feeling worn down and drained, tired of fighting, tired of being alone and tired of running. Swimming across the bay on the Central Oregon coast, I tried again to get away from the law, but when I arrived on shore, there they were waiting for me and off to jail I went. I was in and out of jail numerous times.

In my jail cell, I slammed myself against things, cussing and fighting the guards. I went into a very dark place. I finally had no more fight in me. I cried out to God and asked for a bible, not understanding but reading it anyway and believing. Peace came over me. Joy came up within me and I emptied myself of every bad thing I had ever done. I began to relax that day. I prayed from my heart and was filled with peace I cannot explain. I had never felt like that in my entire life. Lightness came over me. I felt like I might float, as if chains had fallen away.

I was offered probation but did not accept it. I knew that God knew that it was no longer what I had done, but what He had done for me, so off to prison I went. When I got there I began to attend the FITS bible study. One evening I raised my hand to ask a question. What I said was, "I don't know Jesus very well, but I

would like to get to know him."

Immediately Fran responded - "welcome to the family of God." I belonged.

Since then, surrendering to God, I have felt the need to be truthful and to change my life.

I wanted things to be different – I wanted something more. I knew that God knew I was done. Now I have a faith that will never go away. The best gift ever is to know Jesus Christ as Savior. I am living a new life and looking forward to being a mom for my five children. I see life as something beautiful and to be embraced instead of fighting against it.

Fran Howard, founder and leader of Freedom in the Son introduced me to one of the FITS volunteers, Jeannie Bohl who helped me as I released from prison. I have a job and God has given me the strength to overcome obstacles and to continue to trust him. I now have stability and inner peace, but it is a continual process for me.

I am thankful for the everlasting friendships and connections with FITS that are on a higher level and greater purpose than anything I have known before. I know now that my mistakes do not define me and I do not need to live in the past. God is teaching me through my FITS friends and mentors, to accept who I am in Christ. I am learning how to love and trust again.

## THE **WASHING**

Broken and full of rage, angry at a world that only brought me down
Angry with God because He had taken everything away from me
If only I knew then what Jesus had done to set me free.

Alone in a jail cell screaming, trying to break the chains that held me captive for so long.  I felt alone and did not know where I belonged
To my surprise I asked for a bible.  If I really knew then what was happening was a revival.  Re-awakening my soul a cleansing and making me whole.

A spiritual dance between my God and me, and with every tear shed He was washing me, leading me, guiding me, filling me with hope and pure joy.
Not understanding but believing in my heart, no knowledge but belief is a start.
Feeling the energy pass through my veins, a washing of one's soul
I will never be the same.

*Danielle Welch*

## Poem for **Jesus**

It has not been easy on this journey
Walking through the things unseen
When all you feel is the weight of the life you lived before
Wanting so badly to close that door.

Feeling like my family does not understand
Choosing to forgive but feeling unforgiven
by your own blood is the hardest thing
So I cling to a King that says it is under His blood

There have been times I have not quite understood
exactly why things are the way they are
That is when I look up to God
who made the heavens and the stars.

I dance with Him through the days and the nights
Never giving in but putting up a fight to hold on to what is real
I stand with God and what His Word says
It was for me that He died, for my sins that He bled, rose and lives
guiding me every day.

He is my confidence, my breath I take every day
He is my eyes , my head, my hope and my new start
no matter what through it all, He will be there
keeping my path straight and one day my hope is He will be there
to open heaven's gate.

Danielle Welch

"For God so loved the world He gave His one and only Son that whomever
believes in Him shall not perish but have everlasting life."

John 3:16

*Danielle*

## HE GIVES US A ROBE OF RIGHTEOUSNESS

I was born, one of five children, and the only child in my family with the same mother and father. My mother had been married three times. Both of my parents were severe alcoholics. For most of my childhood I felt very lonely because I was mostly left to myself. My life on the streets from age 24 on became a blur. I was sexually abused for several years and began drinking and using drugs when I was eleven years old.

When I was eleven years old, my mom, step-dad and three other family members were killed in a car accident – all had been drinking heavily. My loneliness increased when I went to live with my mom's youngest brother. That did not work out and soon I was living with my great aunt and uncle.

At the age of fourteen I had a Herington rod placed in my spine to keep my back straight. It has always caused me a great deal of pain but because of my drug use my pain was tolerable until 2005 when the pain became unbearable. The prognosis is that down the line I will end up in a wheelchair. However, I am trusting the Lord for my healing or a plan for pain management, claiming the words from Isaiah 40:31, "Those who hope in the Lord shall renew their strength. They shall rise on wings of eagles. They will run and not be weary; they shall walk and not faint."

Drugs brought me to jail in 1976. Then I was in and out of jail for twenty one years, when I ended up going to prison. By the time I arrived at Coffee Creek Correctional Facility I had lost much more

# The Quilt

than my freedom. My life had been and still was a total struggle. For twenty seven years I had been addicted to heroin and cocaine. Filled with the shame, despair and hopelessness that brought me to prison, I felt abandoned and alone.

In prison in 2005 Jesus came to me and tenderly cradled my brokenness with his love and comfort. He revealed to me his desire to call me his own and through the word and bible study assured me that he would take great delight in caring for me.

September 25, 2005 I began my new life of sobriety. While going through withdrawal in prison, I picked up a bible and read Philippians 4:13, "I can do all things through Christ who gives me the strength." I began to go to chapel in prison mainly to see my friends, then one day Jesus became one of those friends. To this day the strength of the Lord is embedded in my heart. I got involved with Freedom in the Son ministries after that, and through their love for Jesus and his word they reached out to me with truth, encouragement and godly counsel, loving me unconditionally. My journey in life brought me to the feet of Jesus.

I was released from prison January 7, 2007 to Portland where I spent four months. During this time Paula Harbaugh (FITS) became my mentor, and walked with me in transition helping me find housing and just being my friend. I then moved to Salem to help care for my sister, but she passed away shortly after I arrived. The FITS family brought me into a new relationship with sisters who wanted to grow spiritually.

Since I had desired more education, I began taking courses at Chemeketa Community College in Salem. Later, in 2014, I earned a B.A. Degree in Psychology from Corban University with an emphasis in Family Studies.

In April 2013 I began work as a Case Manager at Simonka Place, Union Gospel Mission, a shelter for women and children. From August 2013 to November 2013 I was granted a leave to become companion and caregiver for Rosa Montgomery, Ruth Graham's sister on Orcas Island, Washington. What an opportunity to grow in the Lord and the truth of His word. We would spend hours reading and discussing the bible and listening to gospel songs sung by George Beverly Shay. When Rosa went to be with the Lord in November 2013 I returned to Salem, got back in school, and resumed my job at the Simonka Place.

Last year – 2015 I was invited to serve on the governing council with Freedom in the Son.

It is a blessing to be a part of this ministry, and to continue to seek God's will in my life.

I know the prisons are full of women with a story similar to mine. But today I know that my bad choices and life's circumstances are not the barometer of God's love and goodness, the cross is. My passion is to help women who are struggling and to share with them that Jesus is the hope of glory and the only one who can put their lives back together. My prayer for all those reading this, in bondage – whether in prison or outside prison – is that the God of all mercy and grace may cover you, and his righteousness uphold you and his goodness surround you.

*Becky*

## HE LOVES US WITH ALL HIS HEART

# Tammy

There are so many ways to begin. I could start by introducing myself; but I remember when I was in prison how I began writing letters with a wonderful verse from the Word allowing God to bring healing, comfort and peace. Psalm 46:1 says, "God is my refuge and strength, a very present help in trouble."

I was in trouble. In 2001 I ran a trucking business that I had started. I had my only son, Benjamin, four foster children, my sisters three children (Because she was always working they would go home at night.) and two of my brothers also lived with me. I am the fifth of eight sisters and seven brothers. My brothers drove the trucks, and I found them loads to haul. If they were as far away as Los Angeles, CA and I could not find them a load and it was a weekend, they would come home to Oregon. I would lose money because of the cost of fuel and them coming home empty. I would get so upset, I wanted them to be more responsible. We were all in the business together this caused lots of arguments. I also took care of all the children, cooked, cleaned the house and helped with homework. When things got tough with my brothers I ran to the church for advice. I also ran to my parents asking for my brothers to move in with them. I ran to the bishop hoping he would be my voice and I ran to Children's Services asking for respite care.

To my disbelief nobody lifted a finger to help me. The bishop told me he would pray, the church told me to pray, Children's

# The Quilt

Services couldn't find me respite care, my parents told me it would be in the devil's best interest for me to kick my brothers out of my home. I swallowed deeply, prayed a lot, cried a whole bunch and kept going on.

One day Benjamin's Teacher from Henley Elementary school called to let me know that my son, Benjamin pinched a little girl on her butt. When he came home I whipped him. I didn't want him growing up to be a rapist. That is how I had him, I was raped. I also whipped my foster daughter – I don't remember why. I was just overwhelmed. Now, children's services had time for me, they took all the children away from me. I was arrested and went to court. It was a long dragged out process About a year later I was sentenced to prison for 6 years for whipping the children. I was under measure 11 so there would be no good time. That was the last time I ever saw my son – the system adopted him out to another family. This alone was a life sentence I felt.

When I arrived at Coffee Creek Correctional Facility and the cell door shut on me I thought I wasn't going to be able to breathe. I cried night and day. My parental rights were taken away, I felt like I was forced to sign the papers when I was in court. I went through so much pain having him. I loved him and now he was adopted out. I felt that I was lost from the sight of the God of heaven. I felt a hatred towards so many. I thought if the law was fair and I didn't have a record, they would put me in some kind of program. Why did I go to prison? Where is the justice? What is a judge for, when the jury makes the decision? I couldn't believe what had happened to me.

As I laid on my bunk and cried night after night, I yelled in my heart to God, 'why am I here?'

One night I fell asleep and I had a dream. In front of me sat this man – we were in a dark room and I could not see his face – just from the lap down. I was crying, with a loud voice and with tears asked him, why am I here? In a very calm voice, he told me

– you know why you are here – it's to learn of Jesus and His love. The sound of His voice had power and His words hit me right smack in the middle of my head – like a bell sounding from head to my feet.

When I awoke that very morning I was different, God began to be a light in the dark places of my soul. I hated the bishops, deacons, pastors, my family, children services, the judges, the DA and the mom who had adopted my son. The list was long and I began telling God who all I hated and how much I loathed them. I asked, how do I get rid of all this? I know it is wrong.

In a vision I saw a dirty glass on the inside and on the outside. Fresh water was filling it up and it was getting cleaner and cleaner as the water flowed in and then overflowed, but there were those tiny insy binsy rocks which were able to flow out because of the fresh water continued to pour in. I asked, "how does this work?" Jesus told me – the more you read the Word of God and hide it in your heart, the cleaner you will become. You will be clean through the Word of God and those rocks are the things that are bigger in your life and only by the blood of Christ and His cleansing water can you get rid of them. I began to memorize God's Word – Proverbs 3:1-12, Exodus 20, Deuteronomy 28, Psalm 115 and Matthew chapters 1 through 14.

These words were literally tearing my thoughts, soul, heart, feelings and emotions – as it was tearing them apart light began to shine in places that were so dark and sometimes my heart felt so hot like a burning on the inside – burning up all the dross and purifying me.

But how could I forgive? What did forgiveness look like? And if I forgave the people would they still get away with being so cruel? All of this was taking time – it was a process, but one day I told Jesus – I am not going to eat or drink until You show me how to forgive. On the sixth day of fasting I was kneeling between the toilet and my bed crying out to God. If I had been on the top bunk

# The Quilt

I would have fallen off. Because the Holy Spirit told me to pray for Benjamin's new mommy. I still get choked up as I recall the huge war that day. What? Then doesn't that make me a bad mommy? Would that be forgetting my baby? I cried harder than ever before in my life –And believe me, it took a while but finally the words came out - "Oh Holy and Righteous Father, bless Benjamin's new mommy and daddy and bless Benjamin to be a good son to his new parents". (Because of the rape – I was a single mom there was no daddy which made it another huge thing for me to overcome)

Sheila yelled from the cell on top of me - "Tammy are you ok?" I yelled, NO. She said, you want me to send you a hug? When I said, YES, she said, "here it comes through the vent" I grabbed it. I heard so gently from Jesus." this is from Me – you can eat now, you have forgiven. I didn't quite understand that but went to eat later on and heard some women talking about children's services. I began to feel something rise within me. I heard, No, you forgave – forgiveness is being able to remember something but having no ill feelings – you are calm and it has no power over you. WOW!!! I was so excited – so this is the love of Jesus. Matthew 6:14,15

It didn't stop there – One day months later one of the guards slid the mail under my cell door. When I picked up the envelope the Holy Spirit said, "it is time to forgive everyone listed on those papers. It was from the court with the whole hearing on it. I said, "I will just put my celly to sleep." When my celly began to snore that night I knew it was time so page by page I went through the papers. God, I forgive this person – name by name I forgave. If I couldn't remember the persons name God showed me their face and I could see exactly where they were sitting in the courtroom. I would forgive them – the judge, jury, DA, children's services, my family, the church. It was an all night prayer – in the morning God's mercies are new and so was I.

Forgiveness is a great character of Jesus – one that goes deep and wide – without forgiving others for the wrong they have committed against us, we will not be forgiven by Jesus Christ.

What a frightening thought of our Heavenly Father not forgiving us. I thought I had a right to hate and to hold people accountable for their inconsiderate thoughts and actions – The ones who raped me, children's services who took my son away, the judge, jury, DA, the church, my family etc. But all of us will fall on our knees before the holy and righteous God and I want forgiveness.

There were many things that Jesus taught me those 6 years in prison. I met so many beautiful people. Fran Howard is one of those people who walked with me every Wednesday night throughout the years I spent in prison and continues to mentor me and walk with me on the outside. Forgiveness brings about compassion, love, peace and contentment – it also brings comfort. I hope that each of us walks today in the heart of forgiveness. Ephesians 1:16-23

*Tammy*

# The Quilt

*Tammy*

*Tammy*

## JESUS DIED ON THE CROSS FOR US

# Jacqueline

I began my life as a kid against all odds. Born into a life of dysfunction, drugs and domestic violence, to two parents filled with traumatic pasts, lack of skills, and broken hopes. The sad part is that it would be many years before they could get a grip on their own life – well after their children were grown and gone.

Now facing the wreckages of our own realities, raising our children amongst the same dilemmas. The vicious cycle of defeat often perpetuates itself.

My story is like many others that have ended up in prison. Trauma, abuse, neglect, and toxic stress, piled onto more and more layers of trauma and addiction that led to incarceration, and parents who faced the same. For some, the parents were the perpetrators, for others their partners in crime. And then the few who had good homes but viewed themselves as a bad seed, maybe not realizing there was mental illness at work.

For myself, I never really pondered all of this until more recently. I also never considered that the lack of spiritual guidance contributed to all of this – even for my parents.

But, I would like to skip forward to my thoughts about survival. From what I was taught, it was by any means necessary. For me, that usually meant by stealing anything that was not bolted down. However, many other crimes were not exempt and I openly advocated for doing whatever a person could get away with.

# The Quilt

I prided myself on being a calculated risk taker, not realizing the terror and destruction that I was breeding within my own soul.

Most of my morals developed themselves based on the principles of trying to provide for my family and myself, seeking pleasure, and avoiding pain. I had a terribly flawed system of criminal ethics and my loyalties were dreadfully misappropriated. A person will distort many things in an effort to survive because in their mind the alternatives are limited and most of them not an option. It is difficult to see this when you are struggling, always having to fend for yourself, worried about your next meal, and filled with negative emotions, discouragement, and distress. So much desperation that you just can't see straight. So much anguish and anxiety that you can barely breathe.

When I was growing up I never said that I wanted to be on drugs or go to prison. Ironically, I always said just the opposite. After watching my mom, step dad, and many other adults do despicable things in the spirit of chasing drugs, I proclaimed on many occasions, "that will never be me!!" Little did I know that statistics were stacked against me and I would end up doing many of the things I hated the most.

One thing in particular I remember saying is that if I ever had children I would never abandon or neglect them – precious, innocent souls. Sadly, that is exactly what I did - leaving them on many occasions to fend for themselves and to fight the fear of uncertainty. The guilt alone from this made life unbearable to me at times. It even fueled more of these episodes of neglect and exposing them to my destructive lifestyle. I should have been charged with child endangerment. Even though I had child services called on me several times, I always seemed to be able to pull myself together enough to look good on the surface and not face the consequences of my actions. I didn't realize that the damage to my kids would affect them for a lifetime. Strange how I rationalized this knowing the damage I bottled up inside myself and had tried to ignore throughout my own life.

I eventually ended up in prison twice for charges stemming from my addiction. This was actually a blessing in disguise because before that I refused to take responsibility for hurting myself and others. I often blamed others for my bad choices and state of affairs. And though I could have continued to do this, even behind those iron gates, I knew I had to stop making excuses for my actions.

So I made the decision to do whatever it took to change my behavior, my thinking, even some of my beliefs, and learn the skills I needed to prevent me from returning to my old ways.

This was gonna be one of the most difficult challenges I ever had to face. At the age of thirty seven I was still so very immature (mentally, spiritually and emotionally) and was living in opposition to nearly everyone and everything. I felt so disconnected and so alone, so forgotten about, like no one could understand me or the pain in my soul. I felt like such a hypocrite and almost like my life was too far gone to salvage. Not to mention that I was one of the most stubborn people on the face of the earth and had a maniac raging inside of me, known as my ego with a critic as a sidekick. How would I battle all of these negative emotions? Guilt, shame, hostility, doubt, skepticism, indifference, despair, rejection, condemnation, unforgiveness , resentment, self pity and the list goes on.

This was gonna have to be a miracle of God – someone I did not know very well. I wasn't raised to know him and matter of fact, I spent a great deal of my life avoiding and rejecting him.

Interesting thing is that I was so broken and rejected and desperate for anything that could bring some comfort to my hemorrhaging heart that I began to reach out to and for anyone who would help, listen or console me. I knew that many of the inmates were as broken as I was so I decided to go check out some of these bible studies they were attending. It was the only place where people that were not employed by the prison could be found. They seemed

# The Quilt

strange and foreign abstract with a concept that was difficult to ascertain, but somehow familiar, compassionate and willing to share the burden of the tragedies that life had dealt me. I kept going back because the volunteers seemed to sincerely care for me and that what I had to say was important. Most importantly, they cared about where I was headed in the future and wanted to share some things with me that would improve my life. They wanted to teach me about this thing called salvation. They wanted to teach me about how much Jesus loved me and how he had not forgotten about me.

When I was young my mom taught me how to shoplift. She also taught me how to lie, deceive, manipulate, and con people. From experience I learned that the world is full of predators and that people always had a hidden agenda or wanted to exploit me. These people were different. They encouraged me, took time with me, consoled me and showed me how to pray. They compassionately listened to me and often brought gifts of bibles and journals. They loved on me and showed me how to let love in once again. They showed me how to trust. They mentored me and helped me realize that my life had so much value and purpose.

They were sincerely happy to see me whenever I returned and even asked about me when I was missing from the group. The best part was they gave me hope for the future and opened my mind to the possibilities of using my life experience to help others in similar circumstances. To take the love and concern they poured into my life and bless another, encourage another, heal another. And through this amazing act, I have found that my healing and blessing are unbelievably endless. Now I know why they do what they do! Because mentoring others actually helps the one who mentors, grow, heal, be encouraged and strengthened. It turns you into velvet covered steel.

I share all of this because I know there is gonna be someone out there who is facing the prison experience right now. Someone who is terribly broken and stuck in the "how did my life come to this point?" mind frame. Someone who is fighting inner demons and hopelessness. Someone who is wracked with grief, guilt and shame. Someone who is desperate for love and a shoulder to cry on who will not take advantage of their vulnerabilities. Someone who needs direction and guidance to dig themselves out of the murky trench of regret and despair that they are in. Someone ready to change.

I wish I could tell you this could happen over night. No need to be discouraged by this because even the caterpillar had to wait to become a butterfly. And just think how long that dirty, stinky piece of coal had to sit on the mountain side, under great pressure, before it became a diamond. The good news is if you are at the point where you are ready for a change, there are a world of options for you. You can initiate the process right now exactly where you are – just ask Jesus to enter your life. Then take the courageous step and admit you are in desperate need of a Savior. Don't forget to include that you know that your ways have not served you well and that you are ready to change. Ready to listen and ready to let God's love in.

You see, Jesus died for us on the cross and rose again that we might be saved through his grace upon our lives. I know that might not make any sense to you right now. It didn't to me the first time I heard it either. I balked and snickered at the idea. It sounded radically bizarre how someone could or would die and come back to life just to save me. My mind opposed this for quite some time until I began to see the proof of God's love working in my life and transforming me. Until I saw the anger, hostility and resentments sloughing off like old, dead skin. Until I saw my pain and heartache begin to melt into joy, appreciation and gratefulness.

Until I began to feel like smiling instead of crying. My spirit also began to have a sense of freedom and deliverance – like my life and relationships were being rebuilt and restored. I eventually even became strong enough to face the wreckage of my past and learned to honor my parents despite all they had put me through.

In addition I began to adopt a set of principles to start living my life by.

With practice and trust it is becoming like a second nature because it is not just in my mind – now it is in my heart.

It has been such an incredible journey. From prison to praise. I won't try to convince you that it was easy or that I did not struggle with bouts of loneliness, extreme frustration, feeling fed up, or setbacks. The devil knows that we are making an effort to get our lives in order and that he is losing our loyalties. He will send all kinds of obstacles, barriers and distractions. Try not to get down and discouraged because he gets pleasure in our discouragements, doubts, isolation, when we throw in the towel or self sabotage. If any of this happens to you, realize it and get into the Word of God reminding yourself of his promises. Make a list of these promises – focus, memorize, and meditate on these promises! ARM YOUR SELF WITH THESE PROMISES!! God promises peace, protection and healing if we live according to His principles.

In addition, when you are in prison take all the classes you can. Treat prison like a college. You have a tremendous opportunity before you and you don't have to worry about rent, bills or where your next meal will come from. Along with bible study, look for other classes to take and please don't worry about life outside the prison. I know it is hard but there is not much you can do from where you are to change things so work on getting yourself better – work on YOU. You will make a better life for you and your family if you work on yourself while there. So take advantage of this blessed opportunity to work on YOU. It's a gift, this season in your life. To convalesce, recuperate and rejuvenate. Treat it as such.

I urge you to start today. Start asking, seeking and searching for classes and programs that help you find freedom from your errors in thinking. Because you see – freedom is an incremental process and can only be obtained through self discipline, recover from trauma and spiritual development. We must learn skills that help us so we do not return to our old ways when life gets hard. We need these skills so we won't return back to crime when we get broke. So we won't get violent when someone tries to violate us. So we won't chop someone up verbally when they disrespect us. So we don't get high or go have a drink when we feel anxious. So we won't go creep with some creep when we feel lonely. So we won't lash out at people when we feel sensitive or stressed. So we won't shut down when we feel overwhelmed. So we will know how to lean and trust in God and our support people when we feel unloved, unwanted or invalidated. And lastly, how to function when we feel dysfunctional.

I pray that I don't come across as a bossy know-it-all or a person trying to push religion. I have been turned off many times in the past by those type of people.

I am simply a person trying to share some experience, strength and hope as I attempt to convey how a relationship with my Higher Power brought me out of the depths of my despair. I affectionately refer to him as Jesus Christ. I am forever grateful that He showed me the way, the truth, and the life.

There have been many ups and downs since being released. Many closed doors. Many people that have rejected me and many relationships that I have had to say goodbye to. Countless barriers, trials and difficulties in parenting three broken children. Monumental debt – over $86,000. And although I left prison with no place to live or any money, I felt a certain peace and that everything was going to work out in my favor. My faith was truly carrying me at that moment and in my mind I just kept praising the Lord for what He was gonna do next. I also had learned that even if He doesn't do something that I wanted or suited my fancy, I am just suppose to be patient and trust the process because He is working it out. Complaining and trying to force my will on things could cause me to lose my blessin' or my lesson, and add to my stress. I have had to learn this along the way.

## The Quilt

To stay faithful amidst the storm and learn how to keep my focus on God, despite how impossible my circumstance looks and believe me it is paying off.

After living in a shelter for four months I was blessed with housing, getting my kids back, a job and eventually my drivers license after ten years of being suspended and revoked. I now pay $50 on my fines monthly. I have found lots of support services for my children and myself and have learned how to navigate the social service system. I am involved in my church and rarely miss service and bible study. I have completed many programs, learned the value of volunteering and how rewarding it can be.

I have been invited back to many of the organizations I graduated from to be a peer mentor and to do outreach. I was even invited back to the prison to give my testimony and some encouraging words. It was intense and inspiring to share with my sisters all that I had accomplished through God and hard work.

And now I have completed a pre-apprenticeship program and am preparing for a career as an electrician.

I want to leave with you that all things are possible through Christ, who will strengthen you. Remember these three verses from the bible:

> *"In everything give thanks for this is the will of God in Christ Jesus concerning you."*     I Thessalonian 5:18

> *"And we know that all things work together for good to them that love God, to them who are called according to His purpose."*
>
>                       Romans 8:28

> *"The God of all grace who has called us into His eternal glory by Christ Jesus, after you have suffered a while, make you perfect, establish, strengthen, settle you."*
>
>                       I Peter 5:11

May the love and the light of the Lord shine so brightly into your life that when you walk into a room it will light up too!

*Jacqueline*

## HE LEADS US DOWN THE PATH OF RIGHTEOUSNESS

If I concentrate only on this life and how to get through it, my spiritual life will be out of balance and I won't be living the life God has planned. Not only am I living a false life, I am not honoring His son, Jesus Christ. This is what I say to myself when I start worrying or thinking my life is mine to control. By getting caught up with a worldly life it's easy for me to fall back into thinking I am in control. The more my relationship with Jesus matures the more aware of this danger I become. Please let me tell you how I have gotten to the place in my heart acknowledging that it's not about me but Christ.

I had parents who brought me, and my brothers and sister, up in the Christian faith. I had parents who put God first and their marriage second because they understood a godly life and their unity was the foundation of our family. There was love in our home. However, I was raised with rules and if they were broken there would be consequences. I think I spent a large part of my senior year on restriction because I was constantly testing their authority. I was raised in a time when saying you were using the family car to go to the library and picking up friends to go to the movies instead could cost two weeks on restriction. A little like "Happy Days" times. There was no physical or mental abuse in our family. All of us kids had God given gifts and our parents encouraged us to use them.

I wanted to tell you of my upbringing because it's necessary to

# The Quilt

my testimony. I believed I had a favored life. No trauma, no real problems. However, at the age of 54, I found myself alone or so I thought. My husband had unexpectedly died and I didn't turn to the Father for refuge. I didn't handle the loss with Him nor did I draw on guidance in His Word. I don't know why, but I became completely blind to all I had believed since I was a child and I didn't even question why I was heading in this direction. I felt I was to be strong and take control. I remember thinking I can't fall apart because everyone who loved me and felt concern for me would worry. I didn't grieve. Of course I desperately missed my husband, my best friend, and I cried quite a bit. But I didn't finish the process. I became pretty much a loner.

Within two years of my husband's death I found myself in the clutches of a gambling addiction. When I was sitting in front of a machine I didn't have to think about or feel pain. No, I didn't grieve (sarcasm), I just went into an addiction that takes control of all common sense, ruins lives, ruins families, and more than people know, encourages suicide. Within three years I had lost everything to gambling. After loosing all my money, home, and dignity I then stole from my employer in order to keep feeding this addiction. The consequence of my lifestyle was 4 years in prison. As my parents taught, there will be payment for the decisions I make.

There is so much more to the problems of any kind of addiction. The heartache, the brokenness, loss of integrity, loss of faith, and of course, the guilt. The stronghold of guilt robbed me of everything important. Worst of all I allowed it to destroy my hope. I was worthless, untrustworthy, immoral and I wanted to die. I was starting to think the only way I could pay for what I had done was with my life. I couldn't possibly make payment for my sins any other way There were way too many!

Now I get to share with you the gift of forgiveness and salvation. Even though I was lost and in a prison I was shown that God never forgot me. He had never left me. He is a Father who loves us and wants a personal relationship with all of us. Some of us have never heard that He is a God of kept promises. He never lies, never ceases to know what we're up to, always has a plan for each of us. He has made a way for me to be able to be restored. He sent His son to fulfill the promise of a redeemer for mankind.

I came to recognize that if I confessed my sins against my Creator and asked the Holy Spirit to help me remember all I have done, I can ask for forgiveness and commit my life to Christ. I didn't have to die. Jesus has already died for me. I am a new creation and I am not who I was. I have a Redeemer! I have a Savior! I am offered the gift of forever being His and all I had to do was believe in my heart that Christ died on the cross bearing my sin, that He was raised from the dead and now rules in heaven. Soon He will come back, as He said He would. Think of it. Jesus obeyed God's will and died with my sins on Him. He died for the sins of all of mankind. He has saved all who choose Him and I have been redeemed. He made a way for me to be restored to my God. For the world Jesus made the final sacrifice. What a gift we have been offered. Forgiveness through Jesus! When God looks at one who believes in Christ, He sees His son, not us.

The love and concern of the women of Freedom in the Son (FITS) helped me to see and put this into my heart. They go into prisons and share this good news. And what good news it truly is. FITS volunteers had helped me recognize that God doesn't want me to live a broken life. He wants me to live in the freedom of His son. He wants me to participate in His plan for the human race. He made us perfectly. And His laws are perfect.

I was the one who chose to live a prideful life of selfishness, self-reliance, self-centerness. This was not a God problem, this was my problem. The women of FITS are divinely guided to encourage us to ask the Holy Spirit to open our hearts and minds. I don't know what His plan is or where His plans will take me. My trust is in Him. Even if this life has strife and hardships I know that He is with me. His mercy and grace produces love for Him and I want to please Him.

# The Quilt

It's my hope that my testimony may help those of you who may feel lost and broken. Maybe you have found something in it that encourages you to seek the Truth through prayer. God will hear your cry for help. He will set you free from the troubles this life throws at us. Through Jesus I find strength and with my new freedom I understand that nothing is impossible with our God. He provides for His children and that is what He has certainly done for me. Don't give up! There is hope through Christ!

# The Quilt

## HE IS OUR HEALER

# Lakisha

The day before my pre-trial conference, I took the Bible in my hands, and praying as it fell open to the Psalms, I read, "This is not your fight, it is God's." Though I was not guilty of the charges against me, I gave it all to God as led by his word, and in the conference, accepted a plea agreement of 60 months in prison. The doctor later told me this sentence saved my life, and that is true.

Previous to entering prison, I suffered an accidental injury, beginning physical therapy and pain management. For approximately ten years I was on more than 9 medications, *Oxycodone, Methadone, Dialadid, Somma, Flexeval, Cymbolta, Amitriptiline, Ambian, Liquid Ketamine* and more. Medical advisors informed me that I should have gone into a coma and died long before. But before entering prison to serve my sentence, I began to wean myself off the multiple drugs without the advantage of pain management. I sent my children to stay with family because I did not want them to witness the eventuality of my slow death. It was very hard and I ended in the hospital. During this time I consistently stayed in the word of God.

Eventually arriving in prison to serve my sentence, I informed the medical staff that I was addicted to narcotics. Even with that information, they did not finish the detoxification process correctly. That made the adjustment to prison life very harsh. Learning to live without narcotics, challenging, but I was determined. My spirit

told me that I could turn this personal trial into a testimony.

During withdrawal I could barely read, comprehend or remember things. I began to make a point to wake up and daily giving thanks. I would read scripture, listen to the gospel from ministers on Christian radio, and I enjoyed reading many Joyce Meyers' books for women. I read the Bible in a year, and since it was so hard for me to remember what I read, after each chapter or scripture passage, I began to do a summary in poem or music. As of January 2016 I have written approximately 500 gospel songs and 200 scriptural poems. I began to write poems for church services weekly, and other events as requested.

Feeding my spirit constantly gave me strength to live with my chronic pain. I enrolled in different Bible studies and church services offered at Coffee Creek Correctional Facility. I began to attend meetings: AA, NA. Anticipate, Meditation, AAP, FITS Bible studies, DBT, Chronic pain class, Grace church, Powerhouse church, Quilting, Pathfinders, HHAAP, Fame (turning food into medicine), Mercy Corp, Mindfulness, and Girl Scouts.

As I served my time and kept the faith, God covered me—and my family—and kept us safe. Life-changing miracles began to occur:

My oldest son graduated from high school with honors and received a full-ride to college. It was beautiful how my family gave him a party and provided everything he needed in my absence. My middle son plays Cello, bass, viola, and violin, and held first chair in orchestra. He is being considered for an internship at OHSU (stem cell research) and has been given a full academic ride. My daughter plays the violin beautifully, loves volleyball and in advanced classes, is getting straight A's like her brothers. All three of my children are members of the National Honors Society and my middle son has been invited to join the National Scholar Society.

I am proud of the way my family managed to create beautiful lives while I worked on recovery and spiritual health from a prison cell. My children lack for nothing, because what my blood family could not provide, my spiritual family did provide. The people in my family who previously could not get along, band together now.

The blessings keep coming. I am so proud of my children for not using their parents as an excuse to fail. They continue to do Bible studies together. The church provides Christmas gifts for them, and my middle son even got to participate in concerts. A retired professional baseball player became their mentor and role model and began to train both my sons in baseball. My liver began to heal itself from the decades of narcotics.

I may have lost all my material things, but the intimate relationship I gained with Christ is priceless. Material things I can get back someday, and I have my life, somewhat-better health, and my family. God did not send me to prison alone; he followed me here. I am covered with the blood of Jesus who has given me wisdom, understanding, love, joy, strength, protection, inspiration, knowledge and edification.

As I look back on the years before prison, I was not living—I was just existing. I had a rocky foundation, limited faith and absolutely no hope. I have atoned to the people I have hurt. Now, when I am in trouble I do not run to the phone—I kneel at the throne. I refuse to live life as a victim, bitter and focused on my losses. Today, I value the intimate relationship that I have received from God more than anything.

## A **Changed** Life

My life changed on that day
The cards fell where they lay
My trial started the end of May
I lost hope and went astray.

I can't concentrate on the shame
I won't give into the pain
I won't place no blame
Cause there is power in His Name

Many nights I stayed up and cried
Now my eyes are open wide
Jesus never left my side
In His word I must abide

For all it's worth through adversity
I still put Him first
I trust Him wholeheartedly
He created every part of me

I could have crumbled and fold
But then Jesus took control
Such mercy He has showed
As all His lessons unfold

My heart is consecrated
My life is dedicated
A new spirit levitated
sin is over rated

My past will not define me
His spirit resides inside of me
Its like I won the lottery
I am on my way to prosperity

It's time I testify – I am no longer living a lie
Thanks to Christ's sacrifice – my faith I will not compromise
I give Him all the praise
For the rest of my days
It started with faith

Lakisha Muhammad

## My **Gift**

What can I give you women that is worth more
than an abundant amount of money or gold
What can I give you that never grows old

What can I give you that is priceless and endless
What can I give you – something or someone
Who is omnipresent and needs no address

What can I give you that does more than brighten one day
What can I give you that keeps you from going astray

What can I offer you – thats holy and truth
The gift of knowing God alone and give tribute
There are many objects of this world I could offer you
But the gift of knowing the Lord Jesus and the Holy Spirit
  is my gift to you.

This is a gift that knowing you are never alone
Allow him to be by your side until He calls you home
This gift allows you to break any bondage
And acknowledge that His love is always there
He alone can give you strength
He will guide you through the toughest times if you repent

This is a gift that can guide you through life,
and limit through His words your struggle, grief and strife
for there are material things I could give you but
nothings valued more than the knowledge of God-
and to Him alone we give praise.

What I am giving you women is a present
The gift of learning that the Lord is in your presence
This is a gift that keeps on giving – That gives you an
  abundant amount of joy and righteous living.
This is who loved us enough to give us life.

                              Lakisha Muhammad

# The Quilt

Satan gives us justification
The bible gives us clarification
The Spirit is a vaccination
Christianity is my classification
Jesus met the qualification
God loves without limitation
Religion takes some dedication
No need for self medication
Our flesh desires instant gratification
Living water is our purification
The Word requires meditation
Our souls need more than pacification
Do all things in moderation
Our inheritance is our compensation
For Jesus I have adoration
Our blessings are our ratification
Our soul is provided quantification
Living sanctified causes a manifestation
There is no need for elaboration
Study the Word for edification

Lakisha Muhammad

# The Quilt

## HE BEGAN A GOOD WORK

I recently turned 60-years old in prison, and I am thinking, "What happened to my life?" Brokenness and years of addiction have robbed me of my life. Like a ripple in a stream, my life became a painful blur.

My mother raised my two sisters and myself, the middle child. Living in one room, we would all pile into my mom's bed each night and chat a little before we slept. But sometimes my mom cried really hard. Looking back, I'm sure she was heartbroken that her husband was not in our lives. In fact, I didn't even know that I had a father. I had never seen him, nor did my mom ever talk about him.

Growing up in poverty, I worked summers picking strawberries and bucking hay to earn enough to buy my own school clothes. I had my first child at age 16. About a year later I met a guy just out of the Marines, got pregnant and had a second son. My husband introduced me to heroin, and that took complete control of my life. When he became abusive, I'm not sure how I managed to survive, except that he overdosed at age 24 and died. After that, my own drug use just continued to get worse. I ended up doing anything and everything just to support my addiction. I figured if I sold heroin I could support myself and my habit.

Since 1986, I've been in and out of prison. But it was while serving time that I met the woman who became my spiritual mentor: Fran Howard. She has walked with me ever since, loved me, and been

there for me. Even when I would run away and disappear for years, I always knew I could knock on Fran's door, or call her, and she would be there for me. This was a kind of unconditional love that I could not understand.

That first year doing time at Oregon Women's Correctional Center in Salem, a group of women from Freedom in the Son came in to play softball with some of the inmates. This was great fun for those of us who joined a team in opposition to them. At first we did not know that these women were Christians. We knew only that they loved to hang out with us. They were friendly and they laughed a lot with us. One hot summer when we got ready to play softball the guards brought out a large container of water for the FITS team—but none for us residents. I found out later Coach Fran told her team that unless our team of inmates were given water to drink, then no one on their team would drink water either. That made a huge impression on us prisoners. After each game we'd gather in the recreation room inside the prison, and the FITS team would share the love of Jesus with us. We looked forward to each time these volunteers came in behind the bars.

Once, when I was out of prison, Fran and I went to the beach with some of her friends. How I loved staying in a cabin with women who thrived in healthy friendships. I had never experienced anything like that. When I release, I want to learn how to set boundaries and make healthy relationships happen as I allow God to heal me.

One special memory I treasure is the night I showed up at Frannie's home around midnight and rang the doorbell. The dog barked, but no one answered. I took out my cell phone and called Fran. She answered, then came and opened the door, and with a smile, let me come in. Do you know what it means to a lifetime drug addict to be welcomed into someone's home with open arms?

When I returned to prison the last time, I attended a Bible study with others from Freedom in the Son, and, as we prayed, I decided

I wanted to belong to God. Today, I continue to pray, fast and study my Bible so I will get closer to Jesus. For the first time I realize that I do not have to use drugs ever again. The choice is up to me. I continue to ask for guidance.

My goals for the future are to stay involved with my FITS sisters, go back to school for education, and find a church where I can be grounded in God. I am going to stay humble and trust him. I am grateful for another chance. And I am grateful that the FITS ladies never gave up on me. My final day of a 30-month sentence will be June 6, 2016, and that is also Fran Howard's 85th birthday. How blessed I am to be getting out of prison on her special day!

*Rose*

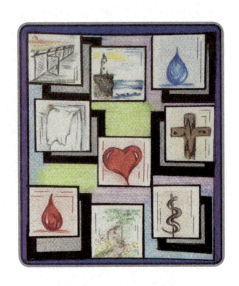

*God opens the prison doors, He is a light of refuge in the storms; He sees every tear that falls and grants to us a robe of righteousness. He loves with all His heart. He died on the cross and shed His blood. He leads us down a path of righteousness and is our Healer. Thank God for giving us Jesus.*

## THE CARRIER

*"For I know the plans I have for you, says the Lord. They are plans for good and not for disaster, to give you a future and a hope. When you pray, I will listen and when you look for me wholeheartedly, you will find me."*

Jeremiah 29:11

It is years later – I have built relationships with the women in prison – have come to know and love them. I have visited women in prisons in other parts of the world. We have brought guests into our prison from around the world – Kenya, Rwanda, Panama, Jamaica, Romania etc. to share greetings and the love of God from their little corners of the world. I have witnessed the power of God in changing lives and instilling within these ladies a desire to follow Him and to carry the message of love to all the world. BUT – they are locked up in prison – they cannot go – what can they do?? How can they share Jesus and His love with women and children in other countries – women who have so little in comparison to what we have here in the United States.

I had never traveled internationally but in 1995 I accepted an invitation from Mia and Costel Oglice to travel with them to Romania to teach how to establish prison ministries in their country. While Mia and Costel would teach pastor's and Christian leaders the Word, they would interpret for me each day as I shared

an hour or so on prison ministry. We spoke in 10 conferences and 3 churches in 10 days and just before I left to come home – 100 Christians had volunteered to begin visiting those in prison to share the gospel of Jesus Christ and today the ministry continues in the prisons throughout the country.

In 1998 I was invited by a member of the Zambian parliament to visit her country. When the women in our prison heard that I was going to visit women in prison in Zambia as well as orphans, they received permission from the prison superintendent and the security manager and began to make items for me to take with me. For several months they made crafts – beaded and woven bracelets, hair bows, ribbons and other items I could carry in my suitcase on the plane. Dr. Inonge arranged for me to visit in three prisons and several orphanages where the gifts were given to folks who had nothing.

I returned home with pictures to share with our women in prison and reports of how so many people received and were blessed. Now the ladies wanted to do more – they had caught the vision – by sharing with others it connected them with the recipient and through them to God. They were getting excited about giving – their stress levels went down and they had something to look forward to.

In 2000 a Tutsi pastor took several of us along to Rwanda. The terrible genocide of 1994 was over but the scars were still there and the country was seeking to rebuild.

Our team of 5 was loaded down with gifts for the orphans – and there were many. Again, our women in prison had given us many items – art work – pictures they had drawn of animals, hair ribbons and bows. They asked family members on the outside to give toys and soccer balls to us for the children.

In one orphanage there were 200 children and 5 teachers – they all received gifts.

*"Like a quilt, God was my comforter."*
Psalm 23:4

We are relocating into our new facility – our old prison was built for 78 women and now we are looking at a facility that will house more than 1200. It is the year 2002 and Officer Richardson, who was in charge of the quilting and sewing programs inside the prison takes me aside to let me know the residents have asked if they can make quilts for us to take to Africa. By now, through my travels I have made friends in both Rwanda and Kenya – have held seminars on prison ministry, encouraged the locals to begin visiting those in prison in their own districts. We begin to network with Pneuma Ministries – Pastors Fred and Lydia Kilonzo in Nairobi and thus began the carrying of the quilts to Africa.

Our ladies began to pick out the colors for their quilts – mostly very vibrant and beautiful colors. Laughter and excitement fill the air as the ladies in prison use their energy and time to make a gift of friendship to be given to someone they have never seen or known.

To our ladies quilts mean peace, warmth, love, faith, a refuge, healing, and joy. The quilt will carry that message to all those who receive one.

*O perfect redemption, the purchase of blood*
*To every believer, the promise of God*
*The vilest offender who truly believes*
*That moment from Jesus, a pardon receives.*

It is May 2003 – our team is ready to leave for Nairobi, Kenya. The women in prison present me with 75 quilts, art work and gifts. Upon arriving we go to the New Life Orphanage which was founded in 1989 by British missionaries for abandoned and HIV babies. At that time there were 80 children – infants to 3 years old being cared for.

# The Quilt

We were told that most of the HIV infected children in their care after a time tested negative and then were adopted out. I asked how this could be and was told there were three things they did to accomplish this: a good clinic, a good nutrition and prayer. We saw it all in action. As we gave the quilts, they were graciously received with happy hearts. We were invited into the housing area to watch as each child had a quilt placed on his/her little bed. Our women back in Oregon had made a huge difference in the lives of 80 children.

May 2004 and once again we prepare to leave for Kenya. This time the ladies have boxed up a total of 100 quilts for us to carry. Where will the Father have us take them this time around ? Where is the need the greatest?

Up country in Kisumu another New Life Orphanage recently opened, Beacon of Hope Center – a home for women with AIDS who are learning a trade, Philemon House – a transition home for men and women exiting prison

The Maasai village in the Rift Valley – where the old man of the village has 3 wives and many children, Lang'ata women's prison (my favorite place) Now there are 5 newborns that receive quilts and the older children all receive toys and candy.

Each time there are different carriers and in 2006 nineteen of us take the trip together. The group is made up of FITS volunteers, DOC staff, Plainview Mennonite church and one woman released from our prison in Oregon. This time we carry 200 quilts made by the women in prison and sent with love. Although they could not go with us, they were with us in spirit. We return to Lang'ata women's prison and now there are 55 children living inside the barb wire with their mothers. In Kenya at that time the child stayed with the mother from infant to 5 years of age. Then missionaries took the child into their homes and kept them until the mother's were released.

Others blessed by quilts that year were residents of the Hope

House – women released from prison, ACHOR Ministries – folks in rehab, Huruma Children's House in Ngong and Thika prison. What a joyous way to celebrate my 75th birthday.

I am now ready to enter my 85th year of life on this earth. Never have I enjoyed life as much as the 31 years I have lived among women in prison and in transition. Yes, sometimes you get discouraged and weary, but as my mentor of 30 years, Kathryn Grant told me early on is that, yes this would happen and when it does we must give our discouragement to God and live on the excitement of watching Him at work in the lives of these hurting women.

The women I have met over the years in prison are some of the most sensitive, loving, kind and respectful individuals I have ever known and it is an honor and a privilege to call them my friends. I am proud to have represented them as a carrier of their beautiful quilts to all the world over the years. Surely they have fulfilled the words of Jesus as found in Matthew 25:35,36.

Today they are shining lights in our dark world. To God be the glory – we are all equal at the foot of the cross.

# The Quilt

*New Life Orphanage*
*Nairobi*

*New Life Trust
Kenya*

*New Life Orphanage
Kisumu*

# The Quilt

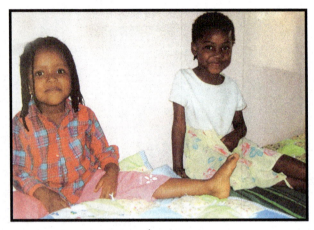

*Favor & Christine
Watoto Wetu Home*

*New Life Orphanage
Kisumu*

*Maasai Village
Kenya*

*5 Newborn Babies Receiving Quilts
Lang'ata Women's Prision*

*The Quilt*

ARTWORK BY KYLE BLACK

# Addendum

# The Quilt

# FREEDOM IN THE SON

# The Quilt

# FREEDOM IN THE SON

## DID **YOU** KNOW?

---

- In 2013 there were **68 women's state prisons** in the United States.

- In 2014 **98,962 women** were housed in a state prisons in the United States.

- Between 1980 and 2010 there was at **646% increase** in women prisoners.

    **Reason given** . . . no tolerance for breaking the law . . . Majority drug related

- Coffee Creek Correctional Facility in Oregon is at **96.6% capacity** (1,276 women)

The United States has **one-third** of all prisoners in the world.

**Have you ever gone into a prison?**

**Have you ever prayed for a prisoner?**

**Have you ever given to a prison ministry?**

# Freedom In The Son | **FITS**

The mission of Freedom in the Son is to share the life and love of Jesus with hurting women–primarily with women in prison and those who are transitioning back into our communities. We began visiting the women in prison in Salem, Oregon in 1984.

> **November 7, 1986** Freedom in the Son (FITS) was registered under the Charitable Trust and Corporation Act.
>
> **November 18, 1988** FITS received their IRS 501C(3) when we opened our first transition home – The Freedom House
>
> **In 1987** we established our first prayer support group which continues to the present – our number one priority.

FITS mentoring program began in 1991 with 23 Christian women serving as mentors for the residents at Oregon Women's Correctional Center.

> *"Christ the Great Liberator has set us free from all bondage; therefore we must stand firm in the faith – of one spirit, with one mind striving together for the faith of the gospel. For we were called to freedom, not that we should use our liberty as a base of operation for sin to get a foothold, but that through LOVE we might serve each other." Gal 5:1,13 Phil 1:27b*

FITS is funded solely by churches and individuals who believe in the FITS mission – we have one fund raiser a year and trust the Lord to meet our needs.

FITS is governed by a council of 10 women who are assisted by 30-40 volunteers who meet with approximately 120 women inside the prison each week for bible studies, prayer times, mentoring and pastoral counseling. Some volunteers work with the women in transition on the outside.

FITS networks with Pneuma Minstries International in Nairobi, Kenya supporting children who reside at the Watoto Wetu home for orphans.

CPSIA information can be obtained
at www.ICGtesting.com
Printed in the USA
LVOW01s0613180516
488730LV00003B/3/P